This is the day the Lord has made;
let us rejoice and be glad in it.
PSALM 118:24

ALL SCRIPTURE IS TAKEN FROM THE
NEW INTERNATIONAL VERSION OF THE BIBLE.

This is the day the Lord has made;
let us rejoice and be glad in it.

PSALM 118:24

And we know that in all things God works
for the good of those who love Him, who have
been called according to His purpose.

ROMANS 8:28

There is a time for everything, and a season for
every activity under heaven...

ECCLESIASTES 3 : 1

Serve the Lord with gladness; come before Him with joyful songs.

PSALM 100:2

Now faith is being sure of what we hope for and
certain of what we do not see.

HEBREWS 11:1

God is our refuge and strength, an ever
present help in trouble.
PSALM 46:1

I can do everything through Him who gives me strength.

PHILIPPIANS 4:13

Pleasant words are a honeycomb, sweet to the soul and healing to the bones...

PROVERBS 16:24

...but if we love each other, God lives in us and
His love is made complete in us.

1 JOHN 4:12

Delight yourself in the Lord and He will give you
the desires of your heart.

PSALM 37:4

Trust in the Lord with all your heart and lean not on your own understanding...

P R O V E R B S   3 : 5

"My soul praises the Lord and my spirit
rejoices in God my Savior..."

LUKE 1:46,47

...but those who hope in the Lord will renew
their strength. They will soar on
wings like eagles...
ISAIAH 40:31

Be kind and compassionate to one another,
forgiving each other, just as in
Christ God forgave you.

EPHESIANS 4:32

Whatever you do, work at it with all your heart, as working for the Lord...

COLOSSIANS 3:23

Surely goodness and love will follow me all the days of my life, and I will dwell in the house of the Lord forever.

PSALM 23:6

"Ask and it will be given to you; seek and you will find; knock and the door will be opened to you."

MATTHEW 7:7

...stop and consider God's wonders.

JOB 37:14

My heart took delight in all my work, and this
was the reward for all my labor.

ECCLESIASTES 2:10

...let us love one another, for love comes from God.

1 JOHN 4:7

The days of the blameless are known to the Lord,
and their inheritance will endure forever.
PSALM 37:18

But the fruit of the Spirit is love, joy, peace,
patience, kindness, goodness, faithfulness,
gentleness and self-control.

GALATIANS 5:22,23

Commit to the Lord whatever you do,
and your plans will succeed.
PROVERBS 16:3

"Therefore do not worry about tomorrow,
for tomorrow will worry about itself."

MATTHEW 6:34

Teach us to number our days aright, that we may
gain a heart of wisdom.

PSALM 90:12

He has made everything beautiful in its time.
ECCLESIASTES 3:11

Be joyful in hope, patient in affliction,
faithful in prayer.
ROMANS 12:12

The Lord is my strength and my shield; my heart
trusts in Him, and I am helped.

PSALM 28:7

...whatever is lovely, whatever is admirable—
if anything is excellent or praiseworthy—
think about such things.

PHILIPPIANS 4 : 8

A cheerful heart is good medicine...
PROVERBS 17:22

Love does not delight in evil but rejoices with the truth. It always protects, always trusts, always hopes, always perseveres. Love never fails.

1 CORINTHIANS 13:6-8

The Lord is my shepherd, I shall lack nothing. He makes me lie down in green pastures, He leads me beside quiet waters, He restores my soul.

PSALM 23:1-3

"The Lord bless you and keep you; the Lord make His face shine upon you and be gracious to you; the Lord turn His face toward you and give you peace."

NUMBERS 6:24-26

But if we walk in the light, as He is in the light,
we have fellowship with one another...

1 JOHN 1:7

"...let your light shine before men, that they may see your good deeds and praise your Father in heaven."

MATTHEW 5:16

In His great mercy He has given us new birth
into a living hope through the resurrection
of Jesus Christ...

1 PETER: 1 - 3

Antioch.

Yellow Springs, OH 45387
Made in U.S.A.